Artur Wa

Just Paint
How to Paint Your
Military Model

STRATUS

Table of Contents

2

Published in Poland in 2020
by STRATUS sp.j.
ul. Żeromskiego 4,
27-600 Sandomierz, Poland
e-mail: office@mmpbooks.biz
as
MMPBooks,
e-mail: rogerw@mmpbooks.biz
© 2020 MMPBooks.
http://www.mmpbooks.biz

ISBN
978-83-65958-49-5

Editor in chief
Roger Wallsgrove

Editorial Team
Bartłomiej Belcarz
Robert Pęczkowski
Artur Juszczak

Models, photos and text
Artur Wałachowski

Translation
Tomasz Basarabowicz

Proofreading
Roger Wallsgrove

DTP
Stratus sp. j.

Printed by
Wydawnictwo Diecezjalne
i Drukarnia w Sandomierzu
www.wds.pl
PRINTED IN POLAND

Introduction

Painting is probably the most important stage in the construction of our miniature. It gives the final look to our work. It does not matter if the model is supposed to be a gift, a museum exhibit or a show winner. One thing is certain – first of all it is us who have to be happy with the final effect of our painting. But how do you do it right? The painting methods and applications of technique described in the book will familiarise you with many processes that can be done by anyone, even a beginner painter. Of course, it is impossible not to mention that your greatest ally will be practice. The more attempts, the better the results, and the more mistakes at the beginning, the less of them later.

Let us start from the beginning. Many years ago I bought a Tamiya Panzer Kampfwagen II Ausf. F kit and commenced assembling. I saw Francois Verlinden's book on diorama construction in a model shop and I really wanted my models to look like those.

I built the model and figures and quickly came to the conclusion that the effect I achieved was mediocre. Painting was my greatest problem, because although I tried hard, everything looked wrong. The model was flat, all details, such as rivets, screws, bolts and dividing lines between armour plates, just disappeared. The figures looked even worse.

I asked myself a lot of questions about what I did wrong and why it looked like this. The answer was simple and contained in the Verlinden book I had acquired. Everything was described in detail there! The problem was – as it usually happens in life – I looked at the impressive illustrations but did not read the instructions on techniques. It was not until I read the descriptions of the painting techniques included in the book that I learned how to proceed to create a beautiful model. Alas, it was only my optimistic impression...

The second, third and even fourth attempts were not what I expected, but the progress was evident. At that time, apart from a lack of knowledge and talent, the task was also hindered by the available modelling materials and accessories. All weathering operations had to be done with oil paints, and the model was also base painted with oil-based paints, which reacted with the subsequent layers.

Currently, when there is no problem with access to acrylics, the whole process is much easier. The acrylic base coat and oil-based weathering agents do not dissolve each other and everything looks as expected.

That is what the book you are holding in your hands is about – how to paint a model to be satisfied. There will be no descriptions on kit assembly. It does not matter if the model comes straight out of the box or is super-detailed with photoetched parts. What affects the final impression is the painting.

My own years of experience, observations and discussions with other modellers have shown that the greatest enemy of finishing models is... fear! Many modellers creating great models realise perfectly well that during the assembly stage, any errors and shortcomings can be corrected, cleverly masked or sometimes even improved. But as regards to painting, any errors for some reason they consider irreversible. There is no reason to be afraid of experiments. As a last resort, it is worth having one model that will serve as a testing ground, on which you will be able to test new techniques. The painting methods I am hereby demonstrating are so simple that anyone can use them, regardless of their skill level.

Finally, a few general notes about using this book:
- All models shown in the book are painted on a black primer base coat, which makes shading easier.
- Oil washes are laid directly on the paint layer, not on the varnish.

The presented techniques of painting, weathering and applying dirt on the models are universal. As for the examples I have chosen miniatures of modern and WW2 AFVs in four popular scales – 1/72nd, 1/48th, 1/35th and 1/16th.

By definition, the book is not an advertisement for specific products. I am demonstrating to you what you can and should use, but remember that there are no perfect solutions. In time, everyone will decide which paints are better, which ones are better applied.

The choice of tools is not very important. The most expensive airbrush and reputable modelling materials will not make you start painting beautiful models. You have to work out your patience and practice for yourself, but we will deal with it further in the book...

Renault FT 17

1/16th – Takom

Kit Description

A kit of this vehicle was released by Takom a few years ago. Detailing is correct, but not stunning. Actually it could have been better, especially when it comes to the interior elements of the tank. It is worth spending longer on the interior, because the kit has a lot of details, but the hull walls on the inside have quite a lot of ejector marks. They should be removed, but their location does not always guarantee easy access. The vehicle itself is of considerable size, which means that assembling does not cause major problems, because it does not have many small details. Individual parts and subassemblies go together well, but it is often necessary to remove signs of mould division. They are very clearly visible on the rounded parts.

Assembly

The manufacturer included a sheet of photoetched parts in the kit, but their quantity is not impressive and they are really basic, e.g. clamps or step fittings.

The size of the model makes you tempted to depict movable hatches and flaps. The diameter of the hinges is large enough to have them drilled and made movable by installing a section of wire. Personally, however, I glued them in place.

On the vehicle's hull I assembled (images 1, 2) I focused on two chassis assemblies, and when I was ready I joined them together. At that time, I had to paint the interior (images 5–8) due to difficult access after assembling.

I did the same with the turret interior. I painted it inside and prepared for painting the exterior. The engine also had to be painted before final assembly.

The only elements that were separate are the tracks, which on the model can be made working and movable.

Painting

When planning this stage of work, I checked out many references. I was looking for an attractive camouflage scheme and found a lot of options, but I decided to paint a vehicle of the September 1939 Campaign in Polish livery.

It is worth mentioning that I had the old kit No. 1001. Takom re-released the kit last year, making it a 3-in-1 version, in which we will find a complete set of decals for a Polish tank of 1939, after it had been taken over by German troops.

I started the painting process by applying a primer coat to all parts of the vehicle. I used black Pactra paint (image 9), which is a good base for further painting.

I decided to represent the Polish three-tone camouflage with paints from the Polish Hataka range. It turned out that they manufacture an entire set for Polish vehicles. This set from the Red Line series – acrylic – is called HTKAS 11 (images 10–15). It contains a total of four colours of vehicle paints for September 1939.

I slightly thinned and lightened the paints (the wash will darken them) I airbrushed onto the model. The size of it ensures that it is not a particularly difficult task, and soft transitions between colours on the big model can be made with no need of masking.

Because I dealt with Hataka paints for the first time, I was worried that the oil wash applied on the entire model, when wiped, would come off with the paint. I did a few quick tests on the bottom of the model and everything turned out fine. Hataka's paints have a satin

1–4. Model under construction.

finish, so removing the wash is even easier than in the case of matt paints.

Once the wash is applied – I used AMMO MIG Tracks Wash – and dried with a hair dryer, I wiped it with cotton buds soaked in White Spirit (images 16–17). The operation lasted over an hour, but with wash applied by dots, it would probably take the same time. When wiping the wash, I left some streaks and discolourations on the surfaces of the model (image 19).

Then I made paints chips. First, I dealt with the lighter ones that I painted with the same paints that were used to paint the camouflage scheme, but slightly brightened with yellow. Why was it yellow? It is simple: if I added white, the colours would lose their nice pastel shade. Dark chips were made with a classic Chipping paint from the AMMO range (photos 21–24).

The model has rather few external details that require separate painting, but wooden elements i.e. shovels and pickaxe deserve attention, because due to their size you can paint them in such a way as to show the grain of the wood (image 23).

I painted the tracks separately with a mixture of colours: black, rust and brown. At this stage of my work I had second thoughts. When studying photos of vehicles from this period as well as models, it can be seen

that WW1 designs with such a chassis as the FT-17 have extensive dirt over the entire suspension systems, hull sides, wheels etc.

I did not want to exaggerate with use of mud and sand, accumulating wherever they gather in a natural way, because I would just cover a lot of painting effects. I decided that the vehicle would be only slightly dusty, but I would treat the tracks themselves a little harsher.

To depict the dust, I used Deposit specifics from the AK palette (images 33–34), excess of which, after they had dried, were removed with a stiff brush.

I also made light reflections on the rounded parts. This can be done with metallic pigments or very gently by the good old dry brush method and metallizer paint.

The original vehicle had no markings, only a four-digit number on the side of the running gear. I found the right digits among old decals from my spares box and applied them on the model.

The model when completed looks very interesting, and the only problem with vehicles in this scale is that they take up a lot of space. Even smaller tanks like the Renault are big, and Tiger or King Tiger are enormous. Certainly, however, such a scale has its supporters and personally I had a lot of enjoyment with the building of such a model.

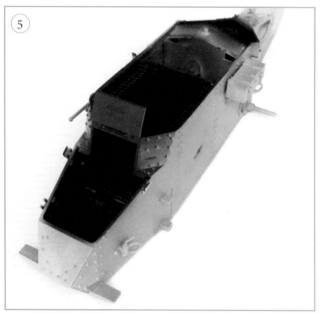

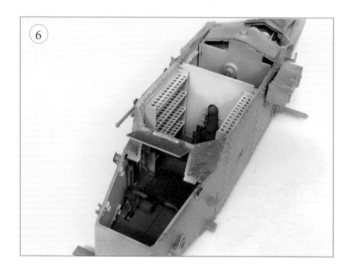

5–8. Interior painted, oil wash applied and its excess removed.

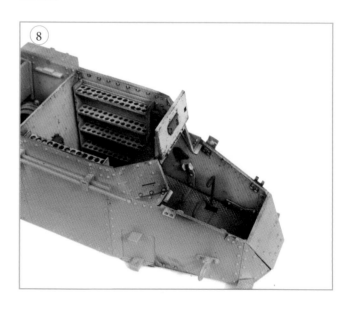

9. Black Pactra A46 primer on the hull.

10–11. Base colour coat.

7

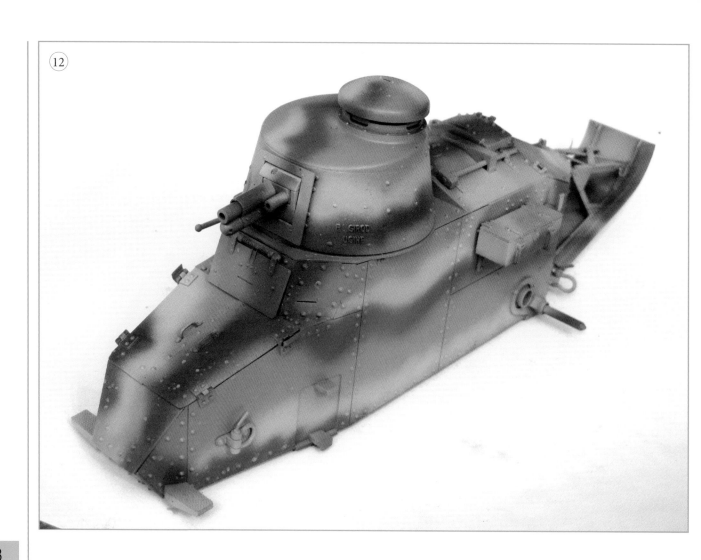

12–15. Camouflage colours airbrushed with no masking.

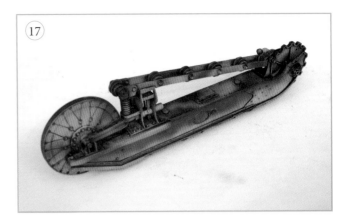

16–20. *Model after Track Wash AMMO MIG had been applied and its excess wiped.*

11

21–24. Paint chipping clearly visible.

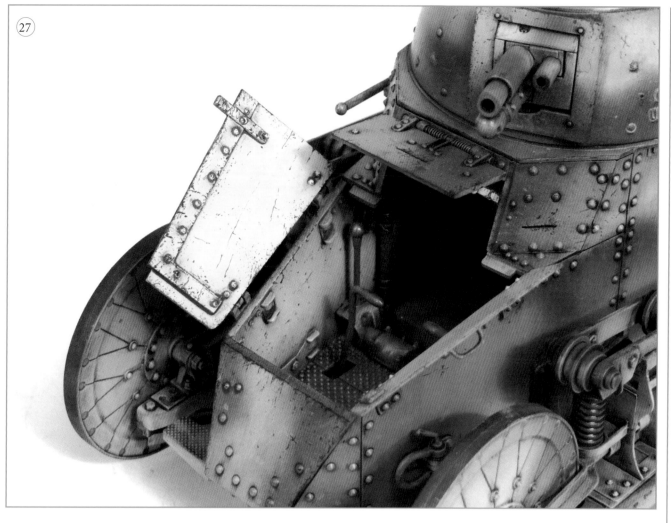

(29)

(30)

(31)

15

(32)

Bedford MWD

1/48ᵗʰ – Airfix

Kit description

The kit of this vehicle in 1/48ᵗʰ scale is manufactured by Airfix under catalogue No. A03313. The "aviation" scale of military vehicle kits is becoming more and more popular in the world. It reaches both fans of the AFVs and "soft skins" as well as those who are interested in aircraft in this scale and want, for example, to enrich a diorama with a vehicle.

I supplemented the model with an upgrade set of Hauler photoetched parts, catalogue No. HLX48362 (image 1). I used mostly the external elements for improvement, such as the radiator grille, windscreen covers and engine. This was a much better option than leaving them in plastic. I gave up almost completely on the vehicle interior, having assumed that after the roof was on it would be hardly visible.

Assembly

The construction of the model was quick and did not cause any problems, the aforementioned photoetched parts fit well, and the quality of plastic elements and their fit was also good, for which the manufacturer should be praised. I started work by cutting out the space for the engine radiator grille on the bonnet of the vehicle and gluing the mesh in place. The model has relatively few parts and it took a short time to assemble. I glued all the parts of the chassis with the wheels, the interior of the vehicle, as I said, was left intact, and the vehicle's cab and body consist of just a dozen or so parts. When gluing, I used putty only to connect parts of the cab roof, where small gaps were appeared. I finished the construction (images 2–5) of the miniature and started to prepare for painting.

Painting

Before painting, I degreased the model in warm water with the addition of dishwashing liquid. Such a procedure significantly increases the paint's adhesion to a surface. There was a problem with the painting scheme, because I built the vehicle in a late version and this is how I wanted to paint it.

Unfortunately, the manufacturer's proposed British scheme is for the early version of the vehicle, and for the late one there was only RAF livery available. I found an interesting scheme on the Internet, but most of the patterns came from restored vehicles from private collectors. Trying to work out a compromise between historical accuracy and what I had access to, I decided to depict a scheme suggested by photos from military vehicle shows.

I started work by applying Pactra A46 matt black paint on the entire surface of the model (image 6). Black forms the foundation, and is also a great starting point for further shading the model. Then, I airbrushed the base Olive Drab Yellow Tone, from the Lifecolor UA 425 range (images 7-8) on the entire vehicle. I painted this in such a way as to allow the delicate dark primer to show through, thus representing the darkening process of an actual lorry. With a brush, I now painted parts of the tarpaulin, for which I used the colour from the Vallejo Panzer Aces range No. 314 with the addition of white (image 9), because the color straight from the bottle seemed too dark to me. When the model dried, it was time for the typically British black camouflage patches of the "Mickey Mouse Ear" pattern. Due to the small size of the model I gave up masking with Panzer Putty and for painting I simply cut out the appropriate templates from a sheet of paper (images 10–12). Then I applied the paint with an airbrush.

The camouflage colour should be black, but I used very dark gray because I wanted the vehicle to show more wear and tear. Later, from a greater distance with heavily thinned base colour, I airbrushed the whole thing, which gave an overall faded look.

The next step was the oil wash. I used the readily available AMMO MIG Tracks Wash. I applied the wash

18

1. A kit plus Hauler photoetched parts.

on the whole model (image 13) and once it was dry, using cotton buds soaked in White Spirit, I removed the excess (images 14–17). Having done this, the model only required some finishing touches. I painted the wheels, wipers, tarpaulin ropes, etc.

I gave up on all kinds of representation of paint chips and other wear so that my model would not depict a frontline vehicle, but was as similar as possible to the modern preserved lorries. Having applied the decals (image 18), which I selected from the spares box, I covered the model with matt varnish and therefore completed painting.

The Bedford model looks good despite its small size. I think it can be a great complement to all kinds of dioramas, but also just another model in your 1/48th vehicle collection.

2–5. An assembled model prepared for painting.

6. Primer colour: black Pactra in this case, but it is best to use dedicated primer.

7–8. *Model covered with Lifecolor UA 425 base colour.*

9. Painted model together with tarpaulin.

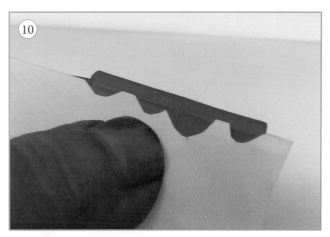

10. A piece of template cut from a sheet of paper, used to paint "Mickey Mouse Ear" pattern.

11–12. The camouflage is ready.
13. Model covered with AMMO MIG Track Wash.

14–17. *The oil wash wiped with sticks soaked in White Spirit.*

18. *The decals on a gloss varnish.*

(19)

19–25. The finished model, covered with matt varnish.

(20)

(21)

(22)

(23)

Scammell Pioneer

1/35th - IBG Models

Kit description

IBG, having introduced the Scammell kit at the Nuremberg Show in February 2018, caused a lot of interest in the world of scale modelling. Many modellers, including myself, dreamed of this model in injection kit form. Until then only the resin version from Accurate Armour was available on the market, but its very high price and complicated assembly effectively deterred the purchase and construction of the miniature.

The kit in the box looks very nice, has a lot of details, cleanly cast parts, attention is drawn to the large size of photoetched sheet and nice decals that allow us to make the model in five versions of painting and marking. The manufacturer also included a piece of cord for the crane jib, but unfortunately it turned out to be too thin and this item should be replaced.

Assembly

We start building the model with the engine, frame and wheels. I am very positively surprised that the parts goes together so well, because everything fits perfectly, and the assembly itself does not create any problems. When gluing, I did not use putty at all, because it was not necessary (image 1).

When studying available photographic references, I found that a small chain was missing in the construction of the crane as well as a metal cover for the rope itself in the shape of a bent flat bar. However, it turned out that making these parts was not a big problem. I replaced the rope itself with a metal one, thicker than the one found in the kit. I used a chain from the RB Model company, and made the cover from the remains of photoetched parts from other kits.

I also decided to install the spare wheel differently at the rear of the vehicle and place it in the centre instead of (as the manufacturer suggested) on the left side of the rear. However, if someone leaves the wheel on the left, then it is not going to be a mistake, because it appeared both in the middle and on the side. I also refined the interior of the mirrors. I just glued pieces of mirror foil inside them. Such a technique gives much better effect than any paint.

The last change I made in the model was making the windows slightly open. I think the model looks more interesting thanks to this, and unfortunately IBG only provides the kit with the option of closed windows. I made the glass from pieces of transparent sheet and thin polystyrene for the frames. The result I achieved was satisfactory, but certainly ready-made photoetched parts would look much better. Probably one of the aftermarket companies will soon release a set of photoetched parts for the Scammell, which will facilitate the matter for model builders, because probably both the elements of the windows and the crane winch will be included. Personally, I count on the Polish manufacturer Part in this matter.

Painting

Once the model was degreased in water with dishwashing liquid, I airbrushed it with black matt Pactra A46 paint (image 2). This method of painting allows for fairly easy shading when applying base colours. By the way, the shaded places we need to thoroughly cover with the black primer, when painting with the base colour they are only "dusted" with heavily thinned paint and thus they will look darker.

The next stage was the application of Olive Drab as the first layer of the base coat. For this purpose I used Pactra A30 (image 3). Then I covered the whole model with a lighter color – for this operation I used Lifecolor UA 425 paint. This is the colour from their American uniform set – Olive Drab Yellow Tone. I use it for British vehicles because of its interesting shade, which after applying wash is very pleasing to the eye.

Then it was time to make the camouflage scheme on the vehicle (image 4). I used masking in the form of paper stencils cut out in the shape of the camouflage

1. Model under construction.

pattern and I sprayed the paint with the airbrush onto the model. I think that this method is not difficult, it does not take more time than masking with Panzer Putty, but it works well with camouflage schemes that have sharp, clear edges. For sure, this masking method will not always be useful. For example, I have never tried it on aircraft models, but for AFVs, especially with round camouflage patterns, it works well.

I used black colour to paint the camouflage, which I slightly lightened with a little yellow. I did this because pure black would stand out too much from the base colour, and I wanted the appearance of faded colours. Therefore, having painted all the camouflage patches, I additionally gently sprayed the model with Olive Drab Yellow Tone from a greater distance (image 5). This is a good way to blend the camouflage patches together with the base coat and works well on any vehicle painted in several colours.

The painted model was covered with AMMO MIG Tracks Wash. I know that many modellers apply wash by dots, but myself I apply it on the entire model with a wide flat brush. This method does not necessitate the use of filters, wash put on the paint itself changes its shade, tones, and at the same time highlights the details (images 6–8).

Wiping off the excess of the wash takes longer than in case of dot technique. I used cotton buds soaked in White Spirit. In addition, when wiping the wash from the entire model, you can immediately leave all sorts of streaks, stains and discolouration.

I decided to make a model depicting a vehicle in France in 1944. Areas under the decals I painted with Vallejo gloss varnish with a brush and then I applied the decals (images 9). Their good quality made it pos-

sible to exclude the use of softening liquids. Having applied all the decals I covered the whole model with a slightly satin varnish, I prepared it from a mixture of Vallejo varnishes: gloss and matt in a ratio of two parts of matt to one part of gloss.

To highlight the details of the vehicle better I used colour modulation. With a brush and lightened Olive Drab colour, I painted some raised parts of the cab and body. Of course, this happened to overpaint some wash here and there, but I solved these problems with a pin wash.

I painted the wheels separately before gluing them with two Vallejo colours: Dark Rubber and Light Rubber, and the dirt was painted with light, earthy MIG Productions pigments (images 14–15).

For weathering, i.e. representation of wear and tear, I used AMMO MIG products, artist oils and pigments. I tried to make all the stains with oil paints, rubbing them with a brush soaked in thinner. Traces of oil around the petrol tank and crane were made with Engine Oil, which I applied to the model once and once more diluted with White Spirit .

I made small scratches and chips with Chipping Color AMMO MIG paint. However, in places where there is dark camouflage, I made the scratches with light Olive Drab paint. I painted them with a pointed brush and pieces of sponge (image 17).

Beside the rust and dark stains, I added lighter discolourations imitating marks of water flowing down. I used Light Dust for this purpose, which when properly rubbed, leaves nice marks of discolouration. With the same fluid, but using an airbrush, I "dusted" the vehicle's windshields onto which I had previously glued pieces of masking tape to the wipers' work areas. Small

2. Pactra A46 black undercoat applied.

details such as chain or rope were painted with a brush at the very end.

After completion, the Scammell model looked great, and its assembly and painting gave me a lot of joy. I will definitely come back to this topic, the more so that the manufacturer has announced two more versions to appear on the market. I tried not to overdo it with the number of scratches, which is very easy to do, but when I look at the pictures of my model, I see that I probably did not succeed and there are a bit too many of them. It is worth remembering that less is more in this respect.

3. Base colour Olive Drab Pactra A30.

4. Model brightened with Lifecolor UA 425 with painted camouflage patches.

5

6

7

8

5. Model dusted with base colour to blend the camouflage paint.

6–8. After the oil wash and its excess removed.

9–12. *Applying decals and finishing details such as the interior of the headlights.*

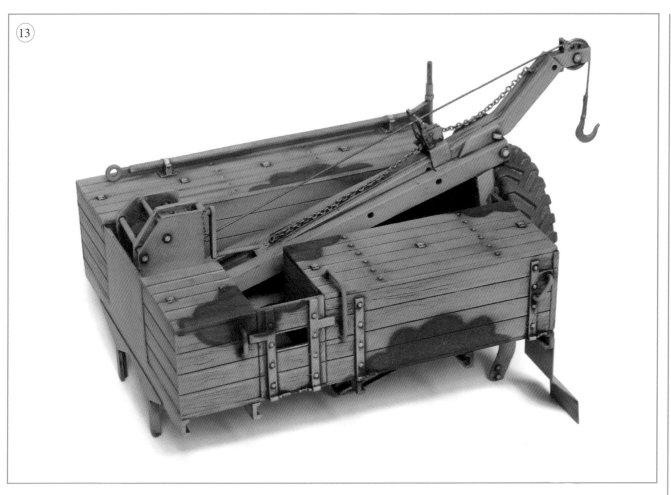

13. Rear body of the vehicle with winch rope fitted.

14–15. Wheels after painting and paints and pigments used for this purpose.

16. *Marks of stains and grease made with Engine Oil by AMMO MIG.*

17. *Paint chips.*

(18)

18–34. Final gallery

(19)

(20)

(21)

(22)

M32B1

1/35th - Tasca

Kit description

The M32B1 recovery vehicle was based on the Sherman M4A1 tank. It was equipped with a large A-shaped crane, and it was used to pull and tow other military vehicles that were damaged in combat or fell in trouble from other reasons. Introduced into service in 1944, it was used during the landing of Allied troops in Normandy, as well as during the conflict in Korea. The armament of the vehicle was a .50in Browning M2, mounted on a rotating ring on the vehicle turret as well as an 81 mm mortar on the glacis plate to defend against enemy troops and launch smoke grenades.

The kit of this vehicle was manufactured by Tasca, under catalogue No. 35 026. Like all products from this manufacturer, this one is of very high quality – the sprues do not have any excess of plastic, the details are nicely reproduced and there are a lot of them. In the set, apart from plastic parts, we can find a small plate with photoetched parts, a piece of string to imitate ropes and thread to make thin rope, which unfortunately is not suitable for use.

Not without reason the Tasca Sherman tank models, as well as the M32 based on them, are considered by modellers to be the best and most accurate that exist on the modelling market.

Assembly

Construction did not cause any problems. The fit of individual elements was good, and the fact that I did not use putty even once during assembly proves the high quality of the kit. I glued the model with Nitro solvent. This is a quick method of joining parts, similar to the use of extra thin Tamiya glue. The solvent quickly dissolves at the edges being joined, melting the plastic and sticking the parts together.

The kit has interiors for the hull and turret, but due to the fact that it is hardly visible after assembly, I treated them lightly and glued the whole thing together so that I could then paint them with an airbrush and possibly apply a light wash, without painting the details inside.

Painting

I started painting the model by airbrushing the whole vehicle with black colour (image 6), which was the starting point for further shading. I used Pactra acrylic paint. When the model was dry, I applied the base colour, but this time I used Lifecolor paints. I mixed the two colours UA 425 and UA005 for a slightly greenish olive shade.

38

1–3. Model during construction.

I painted the model with an airbrush, starting from the centre of the surfaces, in such a way that in the areas of shaded joints of plates and rivets, a delicate trace of black primer would show from underneath (images 7–9), which was to imitate darkening. The interior of the turret and hull was airbrushed with white paint and then coated with AMMO MIG Track Wash (images 4–5), the excess of which I wiped with cotton buds.

Once the base color is dried, I applied Track Wash AMMO MIG to the entire model, which after drying was also removed from the model with cotton buds soaked in White Spirit (images 10–12). I realise that most modellers apply wash using dots, but I think applying it on the whole model gives more realistic results than using the dot technique. The oil wash applied on the entire model reacts with the paint, changing its shade to a darker one, and when wiping you can get, for example, stains and discolouration. Having completed this procedure, with a brush, I painted gloss varnish on the areas where the decals were to be and I applied them onto the model.

I decided my model would represent a vehicle of the Polish 1st Armoured Division of General Maczek. It is true that I did not find any specific reference photograph, but in the available publications I found information that several such vehicles were at the disposal of the Division's workshop company. Once the decals were dry, I painted the whole model with Vallejo matt varnish with an airbrush.

The set contained string to make ropes and thread to create a thin rope. While the string worked quite well and did not need to be replaced with a steel cord, the thread once painted, absorbed the paint and frayed. I changed it for a much better one, made from stretched sprue.

The next step was painting all the details on the model, i.e. tools, bogie wheel rims, ropes, armament. I used Vallejo from the Panzer Aces Dark Rubber range for painting the bogie wheel components (image 13), I painted the tools in dark gray, and wooden parts with Vallejo New Wood.

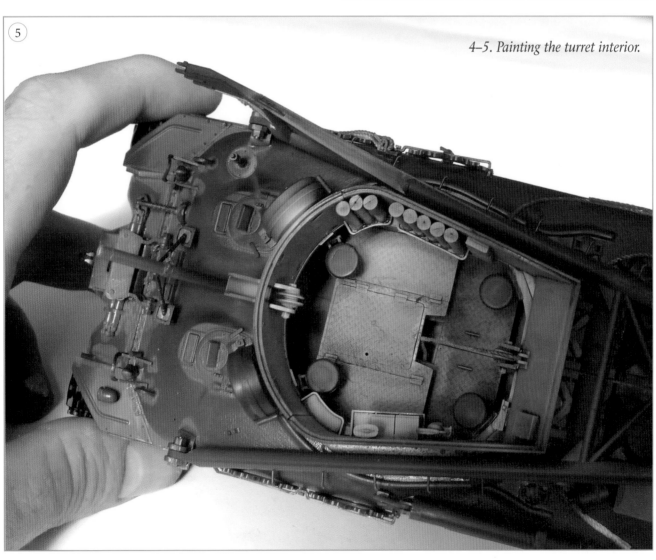

4–5. Painting the turret interior.

The next step of painting is chipping. Many modellers have problems with this phase and are often afraid to do any chipping at all, so as not to spoil the entire previous painting effect. For those who are less experienced, I recommend using artist oil paints – Van Dyck brown with a bit of bone black will be good. The use of this type of paint gives us the ability to easily remove it from the model at any time, if of course the model is painted with acrylics. If we are not satisfied with the chips we painted, we can remove them with a stick soaked in Eco-1 or White Spirit and try again. Once the art of "destruction" is mastered, we can use acrylic paint. I used the AK Interactive Chipping colour (image 16), but if we do not have it handy, we can do the same with rust and black paints. The proportions should be selected individually, when mixing both colours. Chipping is best painted with a very thin sharply pointed brush and it is always worth remembering that it is better to paint less than more of them. With a brush we can paint longitudinal scratches and smaller scuffs well, while the smallest chips can be made with a piece of sponge, but you should do it carefully. Rusty scratching on the spare sprocket wheels was made partly with acrylics, partly with artist oils.

In case of the model I decided to depict various kinds of stains and discolouration. For the former I used Rust Effects AMMO MIG (image 19), applying the streaks with a fine brush, and then rubbing them with a stick soaked in Eco-1. Discolouration is Dust Effect applied and wiped in the same way as above. One of the final stages of aging the model was the application of pigments to the tracks and partly to the vehicle's hull. For this procedure I used two MIG Productions pigments: Light Dust and European Dust (images 17–18). I applied pigments both dry as well as wet, mixed with extraction naphtha, and their excess was removed from the model with a flat brush.

To make the look of the finished model even more attractive, I added RB Model chains. I painted them a dark red colour and then glued them to the model. In addition, I made an imitation of a piece of cloth with Green Stuff, which after painting I placed on one arm of the lifting gear.

Having completed the model, I had to admit that being a very interesting design of actual vehicle it looks nice as a miniature and it is definitely worth paying attention.

6. Black primer on the model.

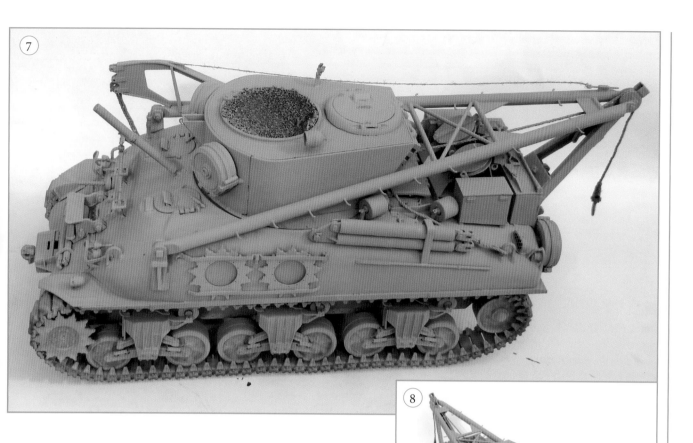

7–9. *Base colours applied by airbrush.*

10–12. *The oil wash once the excess was wiped.*

13–14. *Painting bogie wheels with Vallejo Panzer Aces Rubber.*

15. *Dust Effect vertical stains smeared with a brush soaked in White Spirit.*

16. *Chipping made with a fine brush and Chipping Color paint from the AK palette.*

17–18. *Pigments once they dried, applied dry and wet mixed with White Spirit, the excess was removed with cotton buds.*

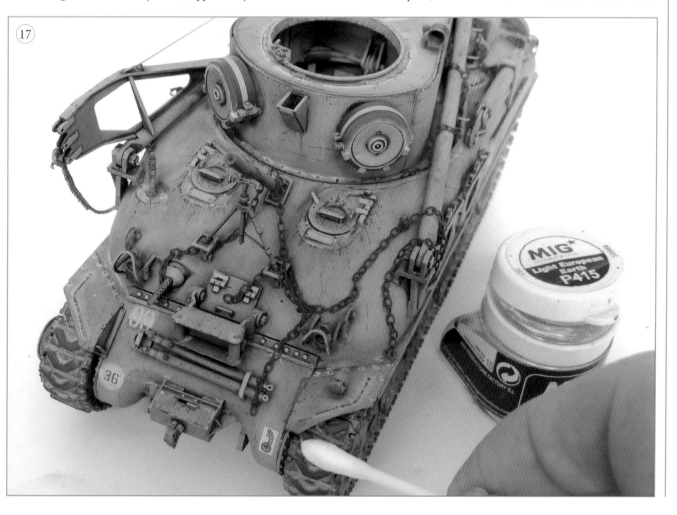

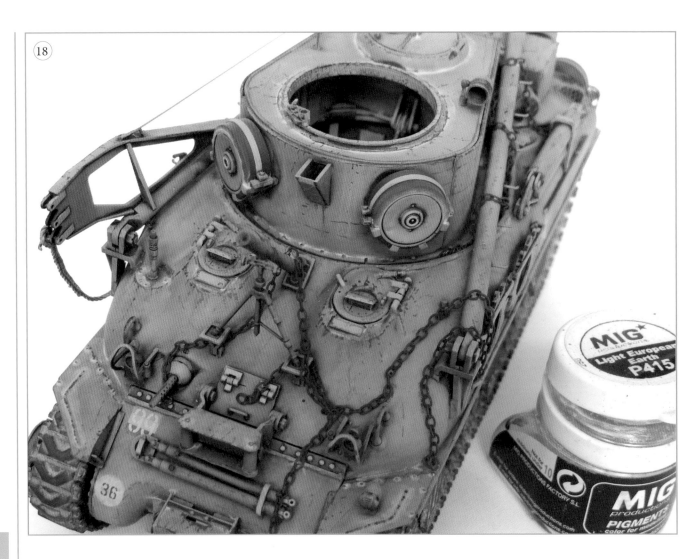

19. Stains represented with Rust Effect AK Interactive product.

20. Oil marks made with Engine Oil from AMMO MIG.
21–38. Image gallery of the completed model

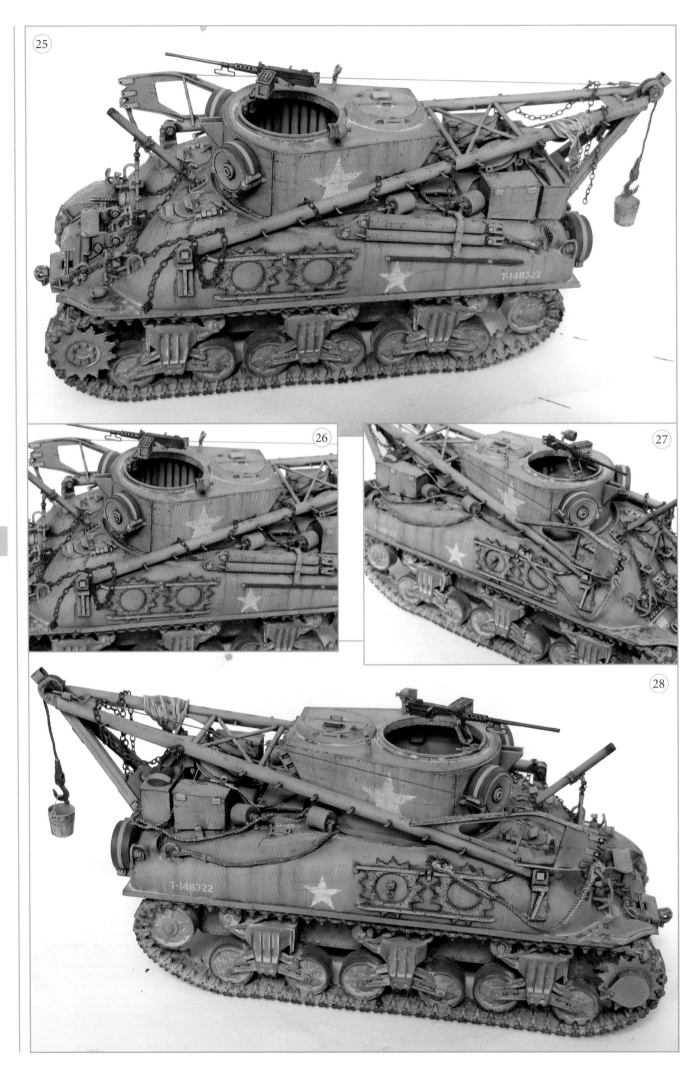

Supacat Coyote
1/48th – Airfix

Kit description

The manufacturer of this kit, like the previous 1/48 scale model, is the British company Airfix. The model is well produced, and the nice details and exposed interior of the vehicle attract the potential builder. The worse part looks to be the wheels. They are badly produced and have incorrect tread, so the only thing you can do is replace them with resin parts. I did and replaced with the MacOne product. In addition to this improvement of the model, I bought the Black Dog set with a photo-etch sheet and several other complementary accessories.

Assembly

Assembly of the model is not difficult, some trouble may be had with some elements of the photo-etch, therefore beginners are recommended omitting them in full, or the use of only the most necessary, where it is not required to fold them into complicated shapes (Photos 1–3).

Painting

Painting, of course, we start with the primer in black. Very often for this purpose I use Pactra black, but when the model has a large number of metal items, I prefer to avoid Pactra, because despite degreasing it can "flake" from the metal elements.

For this type of task, AMMO MIG One Shot in black is well suited. Its excellent coverage of both plastic and other elements guarantees stress-free and quick laying of the primer on the entire model (photos 4–5).

The vehicle was supposed to be in a uniform sand colour, so I painted it with a mixture of sand shades from Pactra (I only had German armoured colours) lightened with white. I repeated this operation twice, first in a darker sand, later lighter with the addition of more white (photos 6–8).

To do oil washes I used the AMMO MIG Tracks Wash product. I applied it to the entire surface, not with spots. The highlights were wiped with cotton buds soaked in White Spirit.

In the pictures you can see the overall wash on 2/3 of vehicle and completed (Photos 9–10), so you will notice how the wash changed the shade of the paint. It became darker and a more pastel brown shade (photos 11–12).

Other elements, such as wheels, weapons and lights, were hand-painted with a small brush. For painting wheels I never recommend pure black, because only an unused tire is black. It is best to use manufactured colours for this kind of painting, eg. Vallejo Panzer Aces Dark Rubber. You can also prepare such a colour yourself. To the usual matt black, add a touch of yellow or sand and create a colour similar to the colour of real tyres.

1–3. Completed model, clearly showing photo-etch elements.

4–5. AMMO MIG One Shot Black Primer applied.
6–8. Sand base colour, airbrush applied, visible pre-shading.

8

9–10. Wash with AMMO MIG Track Wash.

9

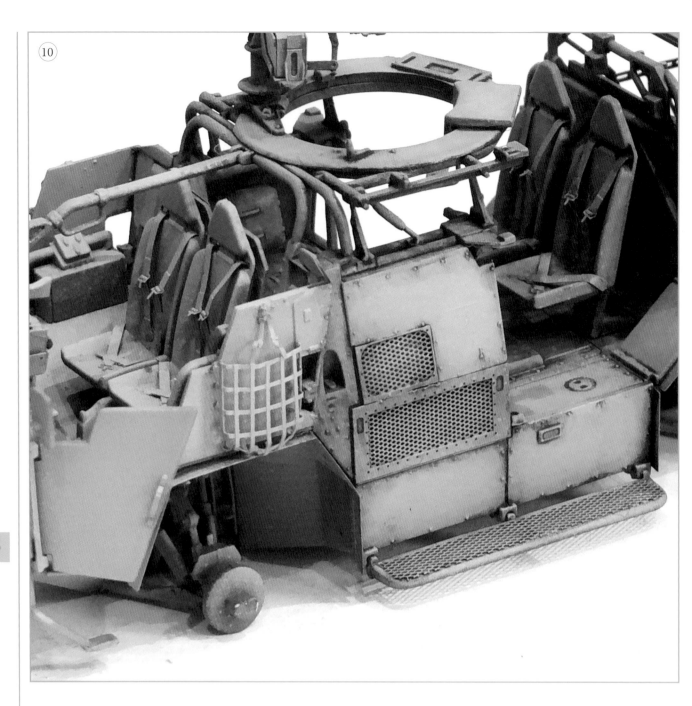

11–12. The whole model after wash and the removal of excess.

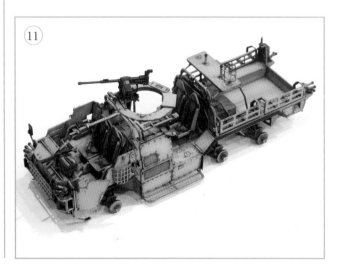

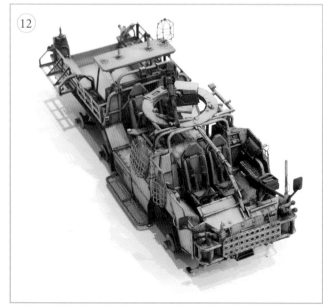

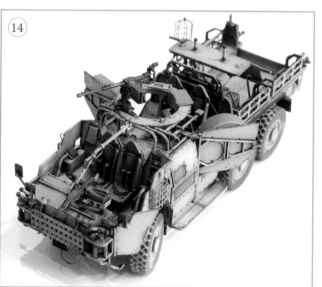

13–19. Completed model gallery.

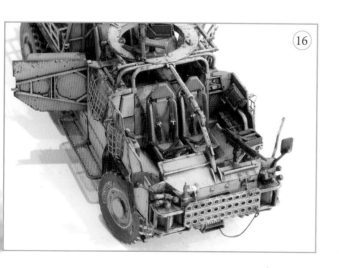

Lancia 3Ro

1/35th – IBG Models

Kit description

I was very pleased with the news that an injection model of this vehicle had been made. So far, only the resin model from the Criel company was available, which unfortunately was very expensive and difficult to acquire. When the version from IBG Models appeared on the market, I immediately bought it and practically the same day I started to work on it.

Assembly

The model was built in two days, which itself shows the good design of the individual elements. Such items as the roof of the vehicle and the wheels were left separate for easier painting (Photos 1–2).

Painting

The enclosed assembly and painting instructions provided two painting schemes. Unfortunately, none of them suited me, so I searched images available on the web and found that these vehicles were often also in camouflage. This was how I wanted to paint my Lan-

cia. So I started as usual with the overall black primer AMMO One Shot (Photos 3–4).

Then I had to choose the right sand yellow colour. I did not want to use the colours for Italian planes, where the palette is giallo sabbia (yellow sand), and knowing that the applied wash would change its shade, I chose the colour from Hataka Grey Sand. Exactly like painting a Polish armoured vehicle from September 1939.

First with the airbrush I painted all the surfaces, but the model seemed too dark, so I lightened the paint with white and painted again. In the picture, the effect of the black undercoat showing through from underneath is clearly visible. It made an excellent base for

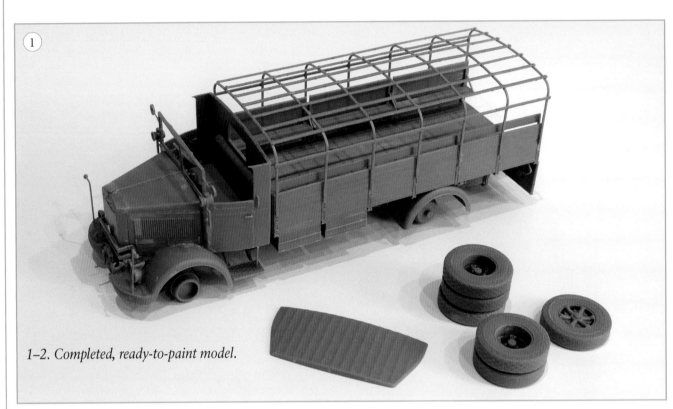

1–2. Completed, ready-to-paint model.

deepening the shadows with oil washes (photos 5–8). The camouflage remained to be done. I decided to use a green shade on the model. I used Hataka paints for this purpose – also from the Polish armoured vehicles set – this time green. The painting was carried out, there proved to be minor errors and corrections in the base colour in some places (photos 9–10).

Wash (Tracks Wash) I applied on the whole model (photo 11–12) and I dried with a hair dryer. You can of course let it dry naturally, but it takes about 20–30 minutes. The excess wash was wiped with cotton buds soaked in White Spirit. This method was a little labour-intensive, but the effort is rewarded.

For painting the wheels I used a dark grey colour, and then mixtures of MIG earth pigments mixed with White Spirit. The excess of the pigments after drying was gently removed with a dry cotton bud.

Headlamps can be treated in several ways. Good results come if you use mirrored film. Cut using scissors a circle of the appropriate diameter (slightly larger than the diameter of the reflector), then cut from one side to the centre of the circle and bend into a cone. This item is pasted into the interior. The effect is very good and even better than any painting.

If we choose to paint the interior of the light, then the best colours I find to use are Modelmaster Chrome Silver and Molotov Chrome Silver. The latter is produced in the form of a pen.

I also added spatter and paint defects on the model. I made this by a combination of methods, ie, some

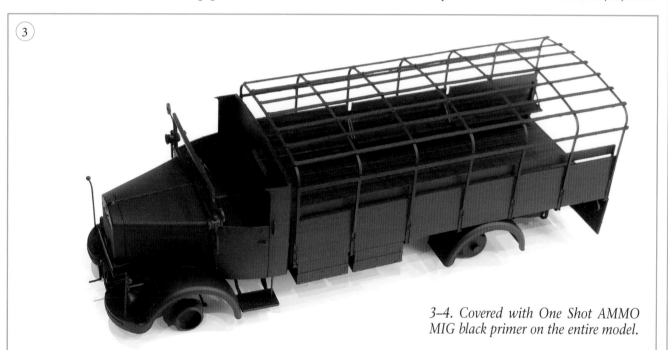

3–4. *Covered with One Shot AMMO MIG black primer on the entire model.*

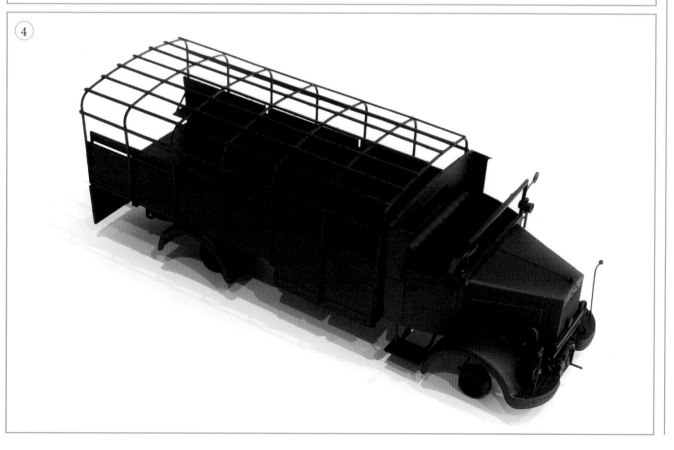

of them with a small sponge soaked in the paint, and the other (any elongated scratches) with a tiny, sharply-pointed brush. The colour used for this is Chipping Colour from the AMMO palette, but you can also make yourself something similar, mixed from black and rust.

We can make very simple use of masking tape, from which we cut out a piece for "the path of the wiper". We glue it to the screen in the right place, and then with the airbrush from a further distance "dust" the entire surface of the glass.

5–8. Base colour on model.

9–10. Camouflage: hand-painted lines, without masking

11–12. *Wash using oil Track Wash AMMO.*

13–27. Completed model.

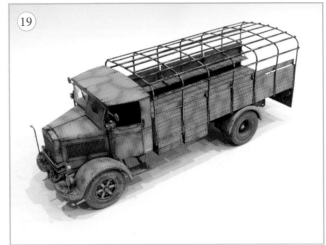

66

67

Pz.Kpfw. II L Luchs

1/16th – Classy Hobby

Kit description

The model of this vehicle is produced by Classy Hobby in 1/16 scale. Although it is a large scale, the model itself is not huge, because it was not a big vehicle. The miniature includes the interior of the turret, and the kit includes a photo-etch sheet to improve the model.

Assembly

The construction process did not bring any problems, but of course it was not without a bit of filler. Due to the size of the model, the treatment of improved details has also not made any hassles. For the model I used the aluminium barrels from Aber, which significantly improved the visual effect of the model (photos 1–3).

Painting

The painting process obviously began with a primer in black AMMO MIG One Shot (Photos 4–6). I decided to paint the tracks separately and fit them to the model after painting.

I painted the model with an airbrush in two stages. First, the darker Dunkelgelb, which was Pactra A104 with the addition of white, and when I found that the finish is still too dark, I repeated the process, increasing the amount of white and painting the main parts, hull and turret (photos 7–8).

The next step was to add camouflage on the vehicle in the form of Olivgrun-coloured lines. For this purpose I also used Pactra A104. The size of the 1/16 scale lines is quite large, so the painting process was not as difficult as in smaller scales, but there were times when the airbrush refused to cooperate or threw out too much paint. It was necessary to periodically fix the basic Dunkelgelb colour (Photos 9–10).

Having painted the camouflage, I carried out one more important action for all vehicles in several col-

1–3. Completed model, prepared for painting.

ours. I sprayed the whole vehicle from a distance with thin Dunkelgelb paint, which resulted in the previously painted camouflage "melting" into the whole, and after the application of a wash will give the impression of being faded. Of course, a similar effect comes from the use of oils for artists or oil brush coats, but the way I propose seems simpler and easier to learn, especially for beginner modelers.

Next process was the oil wash. The model is quite large, so the turret was covered with wash separately and wiped off (photos 11–12), then the hull to the wheel line and the wheels and the chassis also. (Photos 13–16) I've done this because the oil wash is best after it has dried after an hour or two. I was afraid that if I would cover the whole model, I would not be able to wipe everything in time, and then the transitions and shadows would not be smooth enough to create sharp edges. The wash I used is AMMO MIG Tracks Wash. It is true that it is intended for tracks, but I use it for

practically all vehicles in any colours. Excess wash after drying (which takes about 10–15 min) I wiped with cotton buds soaked in White Spirit or solvent for oil paints. This is a fairly laborious activity, especially in the larger scale of 1/16, but it brings good results and allows you to control the entire operation process. If we take off too much, we can improve the piece at any time by adding wash again. Later, the places where they were supposed to be decals, I covered with gloss varnish with a brush, I applied decals and I covered the entire model with Matt lacquer. I used Vallejo paints for both.

Another activity was the painting of spatter and abrasions of the paint surface. I made this with AMMO MIG Chipping Colour and a fine retouching brush with a pointed tip (photos 16–17). I also used in some places a small sponge.

For the oil traces I used the specific AMMO MIG Engine Oil, while some of the rivets that were previously optically emphasised with a dark wash, I flooded around

4–6. Overlaying primer in black AMMO One Shot.

them with a clear pigment (dust) dissolved in White Spirit, and then the excess was removed with a stick.

I used the AK Interactive Engine Oil and structural pastes and pigments in earthy colours at the wheels and the lower hull. All the tools, metal parts, as well as the barrels, I painted dark grey-blue colour. I made this myself, mixing black with white and adding a drop of blue. The wooden elements are the finished wood colour from the AMMO palette, which after drying, I put on the Track Wash oil wash and I dry-brushed to make most of it. The silencer was first painted in dark grey, and then the sponge made the shades in the order: cream, rust, orange. The whole was supplemented with pigments (photo 37).

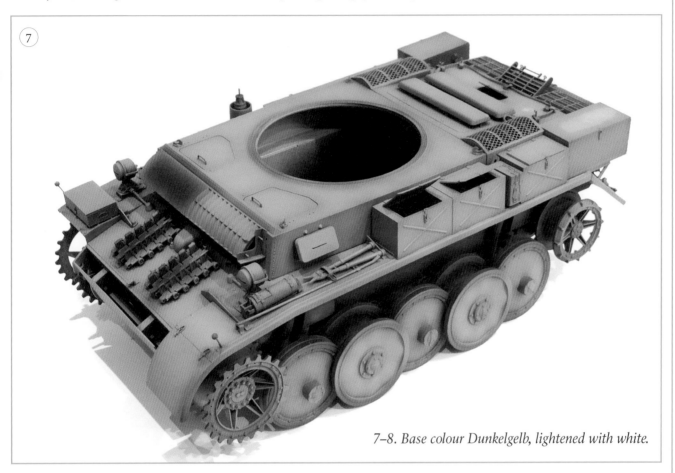

7–8. Base colour Dunkelgelb, lightened with white.

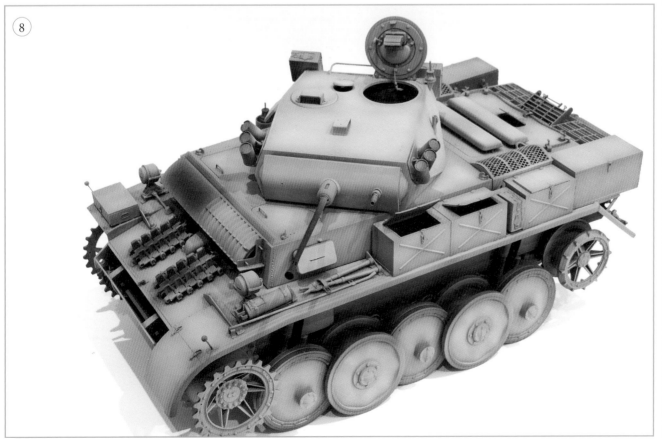

9-10 – *Camouflage on the model made with the airbrush using the Pactra Olivegrun colour*

11–12. Tank turret after oil washing and removal of excess.

13–15. Tank hull after wash.

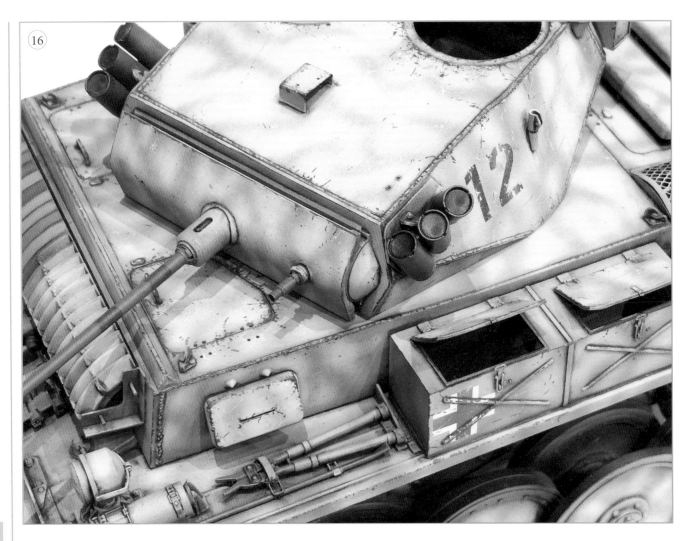

16

17

16–17. *Chipping made partly by a sponge, partly with a retouching brush.*

18–46. *Gallery of the finished model.*

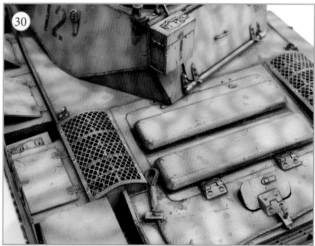

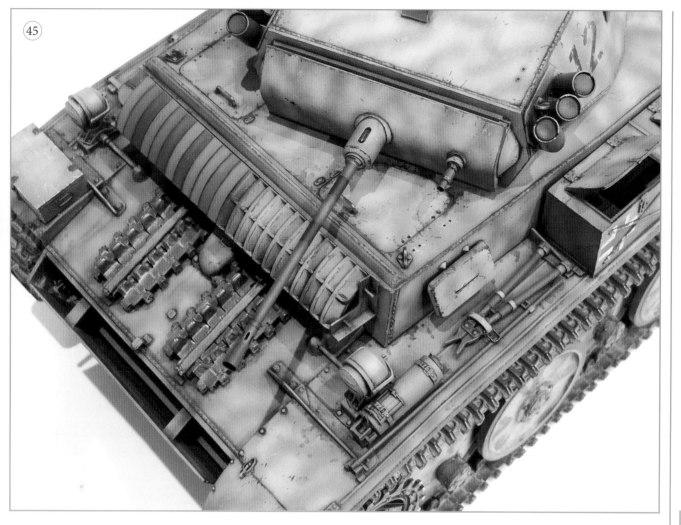

Sd.Kfz.251
1/100ᵗʰ – Zvezda

Kit description

The Model that I present to you is the Sd.Kfz. 251 scale 1/100 (photo 1–2). All that was needed to assemble it was a knife, a nail file, glue and clippers to cut out parts from the sprue frames. It is an ideal model for beginners who do not yet know whether they will continue their adventure with scale models. Its dimensions and simplicity allow you to paint easily with a brush. Not everything is suitable to paint with an airbrush, so mastering the art of the paint brush is most useful later for painting details.

Assembly

The building process itself lasted no longer than 30 min. The model is simple and does not pose problems (picture 3).

Painting

The model is so small that I glued a piece of polystyrene sprue underneath to make it easier to hold it (picture 4).

When painting with a brush, we need in addition to a brush or two, a primer spray. I used Mr. Hobby Surfacer (Photos 5–6). Firstly, the cover with the matt primer exposes possible imperfections that we need to correct, but in this case it was not necessary. Secondly, it gives a great base for painting with a brush. If we did not cover the model beforehand, the paint could be "slipping" on the surface and severely hinder the work. We will paint with Pactra paints (Photos 7–8), because I think that their paint brushes well.

The vehicle is to be dark grey as used at the beginning of the war by the German Army. I did not apply the finished colour from the bottle here, but I prepared it myself. I used black, white and blue shades. Why Blue? When a dark grey colour is created from a mixture of black and white, it is worth adding a drop or two of blue to get a steel shade. Prepared in a container, the mixture was well thinned with water. It should be remembered that too dense paint will leave a lot of streaks and visible layers, and in addition, we can quickly cover small details, eg. rivets, panel lines. I propose 60% paint and 40% water.

Choosing a brush is also important when you paint the whole model. It should be of natural bristles rather than synthetic. For such a small model the most suitable brush with is size 2–3 round.

I covered the model with the first thin layer of paint. You can see that it is not well painted (Photo 9), but we are about to cover it with a few thin layers, not one thick one, not losing the details. I painted the model three times after drying the individual layers (photo 10).

With the rest of the painting I made a lighter colour, adding white and so with the shade obtained using a small brush I painted the details such as the driver's port, and the front flap from the engine for a better effect. This was done to make the colour modulation. By painting with an airbrush, we have a wide field of shading possibilities, while with the brush we can make some lighter elements to emphasize the details and give the model a three-dimensional appearance (photos 11–12).

The next step is to wash with AMMO MIG Track Wash, of course. I covered the whole model with it, as with larger scales, and after drying (10–15 min) I wiped the excess with cotton buds soaked in White Spirit (photos 13–17). Only the finishing of details, painting of tracks, lights, weapons are left. The finished model is shown.

1–2. Model box and contents before assembly.

3. Completed model.

4. Model glued to a piece of sprue, to make it easier to paint and manipulate it.

5–6. Surfacer Spray Coating.

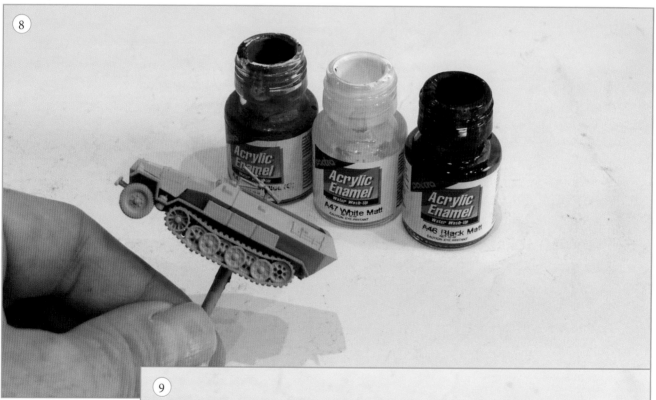

7–8. Pactra Paints used.

9. First layer of paint on the model.

85

10. *Model after 3 layers of paint.*

11–12. *Colour modulation.*

13–14. *Before the wash.*

15. Assed wash.

16–17. After the wash covering was removed.
18–22. Model Gallery.

19

V3000s/V3000 SMM

1/72th – IBG Models

Kit description

I really like the IBG models, especially in 1/72 scale. When courtesy of the company I received two new vehicles, I immediately set to work on them.

Assembly

The basic construction of the vehicles did not normally have any problems, but less experienced modelers may have some difficulty in the version with the Flak 38, because the model contains quite a few parts of photo-etch in the aforementioned gun. Fortunately, for the most part there are plastic alternatives, they are not as intricate as those in metal, but they will facilitate the assembly.

In addition, I drilled holes in the lights so that on one of the final stages of painting was to paint the headlamp lenses chrome.

Completed models, ready to paint, photos 1–7.

Painting

Painting of course we start with a black primer. I used the AMMO MIG One Shot (Photo 8). Then the regular version of the Ford, without Flak, covered in a mix of black and white with a little blue Panzer grey (Photo 9). For the purpose of later wash I made this a lighter shade, because the wash darkens the shade of the paint. The version with the Flak was intended to be in two-colour camouflage: Dunkelgelb/Olivegrun, which is why I covered the whole model with the Olivegrun colour from the Pactra set (Photo 9).

For such a scheme I masked using Panzer Putty shapes (You can use Pattafix adhesive) as shown in the photos 10–11.

The next step was to paint the whole model with the Dunkelgelb colour and after it was dry remove the masking (Photos 13–16).

As you can see, the edges of the camouflage areas came out sharp, and the camouflage itself is clearly visible. Of course there are places where painting did not happen as I had expected it. Most often this is the case in the recessed areas, where the placement of the masking putty proved difficult. These places have been painted by hand with a brush.

To standardize the camouflage and blend it a little bit into the whole, I gently airbrushed the whole model with the colour Dunkelgelb (Photo 16). Camouflage "melted" into the whole and gives the impression that our vehicle was not painted today.

Both models were ready for wash. This was obviously the AMMO MIG Track Wash applied to both (Photo 17), and after the drying removed the excess with cotton buds soaked in White Spirit (photos 18–19). Often for speeding up the process, I use a hair dryer. The rest of the painting is finishing details, wheels, tools, lights (Model Master 1790 Chrome silver). Scale model kits usually have decals, so the places where they are to be located I cover with a shiny Vallejo varnish most often with a brush, and after applying the decal the whole model is covered using the airbrush with Matt Lacquer, also Vallejo.

①   *1–7. Both models completed ready for painting.*

8. AMMO MIG One Shot Black Primer.

9. Base colours: Panzergrau light circular version, Olivegrun.

10–12. Masking using the Panzer Putty.

13–16. Camouflage Painting.

17. *Addition of oil wash.*

18. *The process of wiping excess wash.*

19. *Effect after wiping.*

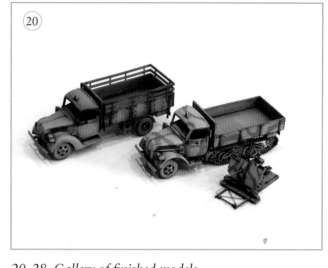

20–28. *Gallery of finished models.*

MSTA-S

1/72th – Zvezda

Kit description

When I saw this model in one of the model stores and examined the contents of the box, I immediately wanted to do it. The box and contents photos 1–3.

Assembly

The model is well designed and very detailed. It builds easily and is ready for painting within 24 hours of purchase.

Painting

I did the painting of course, starting with the black AMMO MIG One Shot base (Photo 4). When I covered the model, I realized that because I mostly build armoured vehicles of World War II, I didn't have the right colour for modern equipment. I decided to prepare one from several different shades of green, to which I added yellow and a bit of bronze. Mixing the colour took a while and it would probably be faster to buy the paint from the store, but in the end I managed to get a shade that looked right.

Using the airbrush I painted the whole model (photos 5–8), trying to keep shadows at the outset and painting the areas in such a way as to leave shadows in the recesses, around the rivets, etc. Because of the scale is not an easy task, but feasible. At certain stages I had to make corrections. I did not consider this at the beginning of the painting, but the model of this modern vehicle has so much detail on the hull and turret that not covering this with the airbrush is not easy.

I covered the whole with AMMO MIG Track Wash (Photos 9–11) and I wiped the excess with cotton buds soaked with White Spirit. Here again the number of details is obvious. Sometimes I got too much wash and I had to correct it by doing a point wash, but fortunately it's not a difficult operation.

After painting the details and applying the decal (on coated glossy surfaces) the model was basically ready. The pictures show its detail and you might think that this is a 1/35 scale model, not 1/72.

98

1–3. Completed model, ready for painting.

4. AMMO MIG One Shot Black Primer.
5–8. *Base colour, obtained from a mixture of different shades of green, yellow and a bit of bronze.*

99

9–11. *Wash Oil.*

12–19. *Gallery of the finished model.*

(13)

(14)

(15)

16

17

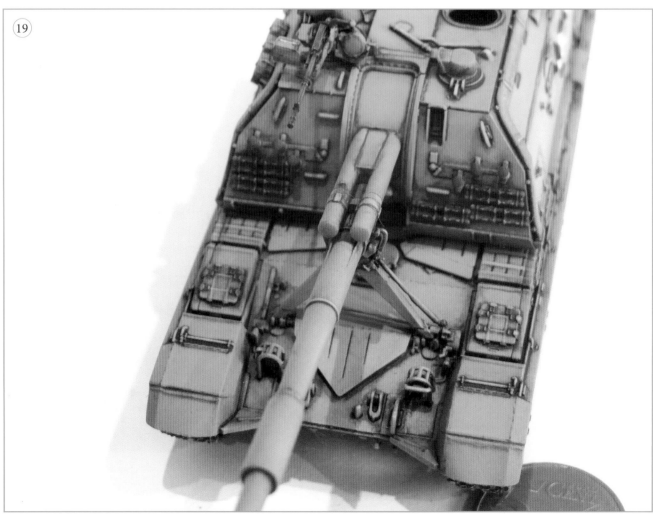